Withstanding The Winds of Time

Reiel Reinhart

Gotham Books

30 N Gould St.
Ste. 20820, Sheridan, WY 82801
https://gothambooksinc.com/

Phone: 1 (307) 464-7800

Published by Gotham Books (July 12, 2022)

ISBN: 978-1-956349-64-1 (sc)
ISBN: 978-1-956349-65-8 (e)

Because of the dynamic nature of the Internet, any web addresses or links contained in this book may have changed since publication and may no longer be valid.

The views expressed in this work are solely those of the author and do not necessarily reflect the views of the publisher, and the publisher hereby disclaims any responsibility for them.

Table of Contents

EMOTIVE

Reveal To Us

What are these sensations my beautiful?
Reveal to us the path for sight
For we are all blinded, blinded in misery

My heart is opening again
For so long I have not felt warmth
For so long I have not felt warmth

These ways unspoken
Written in code
Are not meant to be broken

At Your Fingertips

At your fingertips there, wielding,
Signs no one dares to speak about
Yet there is no yielding
To the things many few care to shout

Let Us Hide

Let us hide

Just another number you see, one two three

They don't care about you and not about me

Ideals of protection have withered and died

Where you've stood all along

Destruction was predetermined my baby blue

To many places where you could find yourself among

You Forgot Where The Most Important Lie

Weep for the open arms so that you mend
Forgetting where the most important lie
Selfishness that is sent out
Show me someone who you can truly confide in

Weep for the open our arms so that you mend
But you forgot where the most important lie
The selfishness that is sent out
Don't let me turn that way

City Air

A place so peaceful

Among the most

Populated cities ever

Escape truly from all

The people who stare

I'll go out with you

Anytime

A place among everyone

Enough space to run

And act like children finally

We break society's norms

For once, for being real

I saw the judgement from their eyes

Understanding everything

As they stared at us

We glanced briefly

Ignoring then laughing

And I was truly happy

Twice Upon A Time

She once told me, you can't go back

So don't go

As I watched the begging

And turned the other direction

Someone showed me something you knew

How to make choices between the

Heartless

Mindless

Given two hands

Which blindfold

You cry

Scream out what they won't believe

Search for what's never found

Losing from the start

As she once told me, you can't go back

So don't go

Bringing down the ego

Someone showed me something you knew

The Thought of You

Looking back
A dream unfulfilled
Mistakes take hold
Gripping
How ever you are
All that you are
A beginning, change
Emptiness ceases
Let's set this aside
Your ongoing endeavors
History that's too old
Comfort to cease
What pain?
Now a dream, your dream
Wanting it to be real, a reality
It's time you rest
Lay down your arms

The Innocent

If I could, I would be a color you could taste
Manifested at your embrace
A color you may call your fave
Dreaming all that you could save

Run away from those eyes
Yes, the ones that pry
Cloak in shelter, hide in haste
Cry in silence, cry with distaste

Protect harm from me
To become aware of the world
And all the destruction you see

Being Alone

What it feels like to be alone
Escapes from moments shown
Gasping for air the breath releases
Left with no one to pick up the pieces
But memories of a time when the sky
Was draped in gray
Things left unsaid, what is there to say

Goodbye to the Wind

The autumn leaves are falling
And I am falling for you
You whispered goodbye to the wind
As if it carried your message to me
Now the distance made itself comfortable
In my heart
And I often wonder if you think about
Our time
As if it could last

Reminded of my limited time
I shake myself of the blues
You whispered goodbye to the wind
As if it could reach me

Remembering You

Strands of hair fall in front of my face
You brush it aside and wipe my tears away
It's hard to shake off the past when
Sometimes you relive it

My heart breaks to see people die around me
Like suppressing a muffling cry
Emotions overwhelms me when recalling
Our past memories
Were you just trying to be happy like the rest of us?

You were honest to yourself till the end
What's the point of caring what others thought?
You exposed your insecurities,
Without limit
And that's what I aim for
Because that is what
Reminds me of you

The Ways

Drunk and I'm all alone
Wishing, hoping, feeling
Where are you at this moment?
This moment where you left things unsaid
Unsaid were the ways that you tried to escape

The Rain From Yesterday

Your pain subsides now
How long will it continue
Earth speaks its volumes

The rain from yesterday holds you back
From sound, softly it's preciousness escapes

Wilting Innocence

Wilting Innocence
How long will it remain
Life continues like this

As if you knew about me
Wondering what's left unsaid

AFFECTION

Longing

Withering stem pulling apart
Petals drift in the wind
I long to embrace your scent
Summer has arrived and us fading into
Your beauty will mark my heart
Forever

Let me love you
I have been yours
Being by your side, I wanted nothing else
Loving you from the beginning
This gift is yours

The rain has dried from yesterday
This feeling in my heart,
light arrives and never leaves
Heaven is
Your beauty will mark my heart
Heaven is
Forever

We Walk This Path

We walk this path together
You and I go a long distance
After a time of contemplation, you will see the sky

A lotus blossom shifts in the water
Rippling
Like shifting clouds
your love has been sent to me by the breeze

Introspection has made my love golden
Only you have seen such a distance
Here our love lasts

A Hopeful Message

I will follow you by the hand
I would go anywhere with you

You have won my heart limitless
Making me speechless

I look past our red line of fate
Wishing it were a saffron violet

Even in the Dharma the Buddha's heart is bright
My beloved, have you seen me lately?

Love is everlasting
Here it has been told clearly

Have You Recognized

Where are we going by following
We are going faraway
Whoever is in deep thought
With unbroken concentration
Sees life

Breathing
You must adore the wind
In the heart of the teaching, there is always what's pure
Have you recognized my love for you?

We have loved
And it is now even here

Singing

Your voice raises above mine in succession

My heart is warm

I feel our energy in waves

I could duet with you anytime dear

In my hoarseness and breaks

It is made all seemingly cool

Our voices die down in ante cession

You always know all my saves

Not knowing what had kept that fear

In my calm voice and mistakes

You say I am schooled

Voice as an instrument of choice

We say dumb rhymes and they are our faves

Laughing so hard it makes us tear

Sometimes we forget our stakes

Thinking over it mulled

On the events that made us sound dull

Now we can express and relate to release in music

In This Moment

On wondering what keeps us together
I make a silly joke and remember
The moments I hold close
Could last

Fleeting
Our photos to view
Changing of angles
What points in time we have always shared

You were there for me

In all my phases
I have learned to forgive
In all your anguish
You have learned to let go

In this moment

Withstanding The Winds
of Time

Withstanding the winds of time
Finding the start to be
Looking forward at another

Becoming like no other place in your dream
Going there, near and now here
In the moment there is

Searching vision is futile
Like sands shifting angles
What colors will you choose for what space

Indigo, Cerulean, Sea Green
Violet, Magenta, Royal
Crimson, Red Orange, Clementine

Like gravity placing pressure
What hues will you select for what take

Golden, Chamomile, Dandelion
Forest, Jade, Mint Blue
Mahogany, Oak, Brown Birch

A beautiful life for who makes
Expressed by letting it be

Withstanding the winds of time

Your Favorite Time of Day

We can take the number line path
Your favorite is my favorite and many other favorites
But the sky isn't always the same moment

Turning, the wisps of air play with the clouds
Like tendrils and planets twirl ever so slightly
Sunlight glistens the stone beneath
The darkness behind retreats
Radiance ahead fronts life

Shadow of hues reflectance glistens from
Rain the previous dawn like drops of crystals
From various parts of the Earth

And the clouds part slightly
Ever so slightly for the sun's rays to
Light up everyone's world
Awakening time with landscapes

Right Before Six

Right before six we go to the dim lake

Leaving the carriage, I dream of better days

Fond of the air, racehorses remind me of an ongoing

Playground afternoons on the swing set

Dawn is breaking through the Stratus

Light shines far glistening through the waves

The lake is no longer dim

Blue filters through the sky in a vibrant ombre

Twinkling stars from the night

You point out the lunar

As I point out the solar

Holding our hands by the soft grass

Our lines match like unmatched twine and interlock

FAITH

Like Rain

Like Rain, impermanence washes away old thoughts
Like Rain, the sound brings calm just does your voice
Why seek protection in secular activities?
Justifiable means brings comfort when hope is dwindled
Seek wise counsel and know your roots in Scripture

Light without dark is like
The sun without the moon
Have you ever seen it in the same sky?
Like balanced restored
We think of dualities

Love Transcends All Boundaries

In the ground there are roots

They reach deeply into our past

The winds of change bring insight

What is a mountain without snow?

Daylight ceases into moonlight

The stars shine

Bringing hope

Duality is fought between choices of the hand

Love transcends all boundaries

A Journey is Held

A Journey is forever held in the family of our hearts
We pray for serenity to last, practice to love and walk the Middle Way
Don't try to give yourself a title unearned

Facing the World Honored One
A thought of your own virtue in need of watering
Crosses your mind like a turned page of a book

Watch the sparrow fly past
Dharma is facing yourself

During holy month, this is my gift

They Say Time Heals Wounds, But On This Walk I'll Cry A Little

On death we lament and cry out in pain
Sorrow spreads with the tears shed
Gestures with comfort
Remembrance we cherish for
The love of life once had

They say time heals wounds
Without love and care where will we be?
Many have helped us with empathy

In a field, I've held a child's hand crying
A breeze passes through and
Dandelions flow into
The air like feathers

Patterns change and the sunset brushes
the clouds a deep blue where
I walk the path of silence

When I Was A Child

Interdependence like a link
Emptiness without what consciousness

There it is, there it is
When I was a child, I cried out
Just like you did

To hold on to something
Wishing your hand was simply in mine
Asking, my dearest, where have you been?

I love you so dearly
I long for you to say it in return
Tears for you

In Some Hemisphere

Self, self, of course there is yourself
But perhaps don't look at that
When you look at me
But perhaps not in disdain
When time has flown by
Between us

Of course you can think of a self
But hadn't you known
Our time on Earth is unendingly felt
But haps you don't know yet
Your stars will always shine in some hemisphere

The Way of the Lotus

Yes, we know our time is limited

All the better to be present now

Ruminating on insight

A Half lotus pose

So you shall balance

Hold steady

Because the early sunrise will

Brighten your day and

The chill won't last

Does it ever still

Has Your Faith Been Hidden?

This scenery is

Not lasting

Land today is sea tomorrow

Everlasting is the Pure land in Heaven

Has your faith been hidden?

Bright is the light of the divine

Remembering, dedicating,

Lighting the way of the lotus

My Way To You

O Rising sun, O rising stars
Planetary arrays, the galaxy's amaze
At night I dream
If the moon could be brighter,
Shine its way to
Our love's last calling
Autumn seasons turn to winter
Parting
When we will see last
Our way to each other
My way to
You

Childhood Admiration

Sitting across from you

It is terribly difficult to focus

Then you sit behind me, and I'm left to guess

Where you have gone

Here to think of menial seniority,

Like what level

But when we are at a challenge

You test my resolve

I finally break

Sight on scripture and of silence

Distracted

I see now quiet is best

As this practice is ours and

Underminingly Necessary

A Gift

The drum will sound when it sounds

The bell will resonate when it resonates

Let it ripple through your core

Inviting the senses

We are

Said together in unison, a lasting mantra

Every Sanskrit name I've ever recalled

Incanting and invoking

Passing by the temple grounds to offer

Respect to my parents

A gift of a rose I will pin

Upon the lapel of my beloved

New Year's Day

Red on red and red on gold
Lucky money for you and me
No matter who's younger we'll
Break boundaries
This is a life worth celebrating
I wish for you love
Lasting all bounds

You Lose On Silence and Smile Regardless

Bowing in respect to the Buddha
We listen as the bell dissipates
Quietude guided the meditation
You lose on silence and smile regardless
To answer your question I pause

Waiting is good for patience
It may also imply knowledge
When those who listen clear enough falter
They practice enough to understand

With jewel holding hands of method and wisdom
You search and ask, 'where is insight?'
That is Dharma,
You see

Self- esteem

All that you are
All that you will be
Underneath the desperation
Hidden esteem will be uprooted

Shown for whom to gather
Or you to expose your introvert
While the extrovert is waiting for you to
Join him at a party

But nobody cared
But nobody cared

But somebody did
And somebody will
So you will too
Just
Care

The Cello's Melody

The suffering of change
Interrupts your evening
Like an illness down to your core
We take it one moment at a time

Strumming with the bow
The cello's melody
Drifts out the open window
What melancholy

Holding the oak leaf to the trunk
Has autumn begun
On wholesome days
We look to the western sky

Pray for a hushed cry
Breaking
Yet you feel like
Cold rain
On who's missing
When the light has come and gone

We rejoice in all good things said and done

Fill our prayers with words of ancient past

The sacred message has befallen the voice of an angelic grace

Let it raise up

Hear the calling

Find our place of worship

In times lost

And healing to those we wish to believe and see

So that they may be saved when the time has come to be

DEDICATION

A Memory of a Soldier

Patriotic days go by and
I drift off in reminiscence
Holding a miniature flag
I think of
A storm flag folding instead
With pride and To The Colors
I salute

For Our Service Members

Formation before the march
We worked with hard dedication
All of our service
Amounted to honor
In the extreme weather
Our complaints shrink to nothing in training
Thinking back to days that we watched turn into
The darkest nights
Folding up the flag
Hearing the twenty-one gun salute
And carrying our fallen comrade
We'll always have you at home base

Love Away

When will you come home to me?
Missing the sound of your heartbeat I
Pace back and forth in despair

Candles flicker in the nighttime
Home isn't the same without you

On better days we're
Dancing at twilight and I'm twirling in velvet
At a military ball, blushing

Setting down our photo
I can't help but to dwell,
When will you come home to me?

Love I Will

Love I will
Paint day and night
With colors colliding
Dependant on my feelings
For you

Love I will
Gift you a ballad
The thrill of a crescendo to hear
When you grow tired, old and weak

Love I will
Read you a poem
Remind you of our favorite past times
Be there for you when ill
And look at you as we did in our youth
Just to get lost
In your eyes
Because
Love I will love

Down Like This

A feather floats away from me to you
It's strange how days from then you were on dive
I pulled my hand from your hold
We weren't supposed to break down like this

Heaven's will left on unsaid
I pulled your hold for me away
Wishing you'd asked for me to stay
It's strange how weeks from then you were on dive

Crash into the waves
And ripple through to me
I shouted, I love you
The words trailed off alone

Looking now and then
It's strange how years from then you were on dive
We weren't supposed to break down like this
I thought we were going to make it

Falling apart, I just can't take this

A Feeling

We go
Around and around again
I just wanted to see you smile
I just wanted to hear you laugh

It's like a curse
And I dread it
You're unresponsive
And I can't take it
Will this even mean anything for you?

Because a maybe feeling
Is better than
Feeling
A nothing feeling

Dawn to Dusk

The sweltering heat has made me value ice
Days without we value minty candy
In the desert we always look for shade
And avoid scorching metal

Your M4 is your best friend
Letters from home we hope for
Nights without we persevere on missions
In the desert we look for safety
And avoid sirens wailing

The one hundred twenty degree temp has made me wish for AC
Running in sand from dawn to dusk
The storm has brought grains in every inch of my being
Wishing for home like never before
On our journey in the Middle East

In The Frigid Cold

In the frigid cold we all run to our destinations
With purpose in mind, we rarely go at lesiure
Before the flag retreats we honor the fallen

Embracing the cold has us shiver less
I walk out in snow to stay alert
The flybys makes us pause between sentences
We thank God for the Airforce
And laugh at escalated orders
That need shouting among the best aircraft
In foreign skies

Timing the First Sergeant for fun
We bet on timestamps and watches
Wondering where the comadre went
When our orders are to return home
While others choose to extend

With winter's harsh weathering, was our
Defense against the North Korean regimen
In the frigid cold

Your Sunken Ship

Red skies have dawned
High tide on your cold waters
My hands have gone numb
Flipping through your unsent letters
Kept safe in the yacht docked by the pier
Discovered when you disappeared
On frail acts of years passing

Deployment

Running with no end in sight
Even in the dry cracked earth
Sand ridden dessert
You will find me on solo missions

Air hangars and connex trailers
Ever searching for shields
From sandstorms and the scalding sun

Thanking God for care packages
When scarcity has reached our base
And heat wave slums
Bring our eyes to nowhere other than home

LAMENT

Graveyard

I went to the graveyard
The ground and sky was bleak
My bones grow weak with age
Entering the past, pass by the gates
You'll seek for me
Don't cross the toppling stone
Morbida is her name
The Hell realms open for skull lady
If you go there, yourself is to blame
And you'll owe hell money on the daily

I Feel Numb When You're Gone

I feel numb when you're gone

All of my regrets of time past

I wish our time would have lasted

A head full of complaints

Puts me in last place

Eyes puffy, I want to relive parts of our youth

All the angles of your obtuse

I don't want to give you advice

I just

Want you here

Dear Lienna

Your smile was all I was waiting to see
And for you to love yourself
To never let go of that

The hours pass by in my solitude
I just sit here and write
Feeling pathetically burdensome
Cowering because you were the one
who taught me to be myself
Still shying away from my revealed truths

How much I loved you Lienna
I poured my energy into my journey
While barely having enough for you

She shunned me a perfectionist in my art
While I called her my favorite inventor
We had our world creative

If All Else Fails

Even when things don't work out
You learn to do better
To rest
To listen
To apologize

You can ask,
What is it to forgive?
For oneself and another
To finally let go and
To love

Your Greatest Gift

You look to me like a pillar
Accepting me and my troublesome ways
Always seeing the beauty in things
Your greatest gift was your time for me

I falter thinking about past days
Nights distilled with your company
Alone now without your companionship
Your kind eyes and worry is what I miss to have had

Weathering Storms

Twirled hair in tropical orchids
Roots out, no white strands
Sleek black dress white slit
Pale skin in a gothic hue

Rain sun or shine
Dark fog or mix
You've weathered a storm with me
You've weathered a storm without me

Siding with the fallen angels and
Claiming death by your own hands
God shall accept your reckless sickness
Repentance in purgatory has done its own bidding

Feathers flow in the wind
That changes directions at moonlight in your passing.

In Memory Of

She loved lilac roses
And ice cream green tea on occasions
I am left here alone to offer them by her photograph
Writing pages of her, for her
In my memento mori

Couldn't find the poems written in her youth
Instead I came across a notebook of feelings
Although we have regrettably burned some history
In my memento mori
I say that this is enough

He breathed fresh air into my lungs
Hoping my tears of pain will vanish

I gifted my expression in artwork
Opening up a world of imagination for him

He suffered on the battlefield
Losing his brothers in arms that were once by his side

In his last moments I held his hands with a plea
For vanquishing the darkness that overtook his nights

I pray to the heavens for sacrament
Hoping his midnight tremors would fade

As he joined the ranks of knights
Laid down to rest

On the fields of bright light
I saw a shooting star
Sixteen

I fold paper cranes and colorful stars
Just as you did when we were young
Wishing they were enough to come true
To bring back the parts of you that is gone

My heart is torn in two
Thinking of the days I spent with you
Sadness falls from my eyes in drops
Emotions like water flowing through

Heavy branches break in the flames
Papers light up burning a instant red-orange
Faint words appear momentarily before their final endings
Sepia papers lit up to floating ashes in the heat
Secrets forever gone on a November day

Everything with meaning must fade
Memories of old and misery too
Up in smoke twirling in the air
The sentch of firewood on a cold winter
Bringing back the moment of letting go
Of years unspoken but written

Something Strong

Dull eyes on a dreary Monday
Exchanges of grief between me and you
Asking for a glass of ice
Maybe this will have you unclench your fists
From being unable to prevent this

I poured the caramel colored liquid slowly
You pass on the Coca cola
We shoot billiards in motions
Listening to a stranger's selection on the music box
Another day with whiskey on the rocks

You leaned forward towards my heart
Did you miss me?
Whispering, 'a lot'
While you were gone there was so much in need

Visiting me in dreams
Lucid as can be
Creating laughable internet memes
There was so much to see

While you were alive
You breathed in so much life in me
In death was there demise
Broken down and bent to the knees

In our prayers your love will always live on
Your visions of the future were so honest and humble
If your life could last eon
Hardly a plan for yourself you'd make,
but even the thoughts of others in a faltering stumble

Your being reached far through me
Your being reached far through for him to see

In the wake of the funeral chants

Tears fall for you while I held you secure

I knew you would have it in you to forgive me

But could I forgive myself for turning away this year

Tragedy has befallen

One beautiful autumn stricken

The frigid wind a reminder of the cold I felt from your illness

Must I remind myself of faults and flaws

When we know you're not here to defend them?

Your sadness becomes my own sadness

I wish I had spoken to you about

My wishes fall with aching heart

Like the petals fall from the roses

Gifted to you

The remainder of days where you stood by my side

Become absent with longing

I cherished you with all of my being

With love like it was and as it is, always

The flame of your zippo has left a scent of butane

The click shut of metal breaks the silence in-between us

Smoke has dampened my hair

With your last inhale of a cigarette

You mouthed an 'o'

And a ring escapes your mouth

On nights like these, the parties were well overdone

And we escaped to the back where

Our stance was the usual

The oval ring of smoke dissipates above me

As if a halo has fallen in reverse

The angel in me on your right side

Ready to battle with you

So any topic of discussion will do

Blinking off in the distance

You begin our conversations

In secrecy

Scattering petals

On gun metal black

It's contrast seeks subtlety

Behind locked hearts and a will for revenge

Biting the bitterness on edge

The clock strikes eleven

Times are harsh and the battle harsher

The eve of your bruising is daunting

Left with years of my haunting

Justifiable means carry out to your suffering

Where in honest dreams you have never existed

Gone by my own hands

Mourning

I am told to lay your picture down
I simply can not
These days, I've watched years go by
Cry to your shadow
And embody the pain that was yours

Apart of you is with me always

Well into our birthday we laughed
What was to be the last
Our final goodbyes

Your smiling face I should remember
Apart from the strife of yesteryear
To embrace the pain that was yours
Left here for me
While you have gone away
But
Apart of you is with me always

He Was The Type

He was the type two
Page turner running to the edge of his speech
Towards the cliff hanger

Unedited edition
Not enough erase on typewriter setting
Who made the words count

Hands tangled through my hair
Plans up in the air
Rushing towards a beginning that was an end

My baby with the golden heart
Center aim with a dart
Thrown into a moment of bliss
On every take

Missing By My Side

In a cold dim lit room
The draft brings shivers through every nerve
And I'm wishing for cashmere

Waiting for December's stars to align
The last eclipse of the year
Reminds me of the solar one we spent
With silly glasses

Our steps embedded on the grounds surrounded by
Books of old and new
And I'm missing you

We might not know where our journey is headed
What paths are turning the bend
However I am sure
You'll visit in my sweet dreaming

When I awake, know that
You'll always be missing by my side

I need you like water to a rose

Like earth to roots

Like heat from the sun

And air to our being

Because you are my gift sent from heaven

In death, I wait for trials at the gate

You're my only savior from ill fate

In life, I offer my time for your smiles

Our turmoils won and lost

On battlefields of grey

Streaks of colors come what may

The preciousness that we cared for

Grow to be intangible

As things wither away

And how we may falter,

How we may break,

Love prevails

And then it

Withstands the winds of time

About The Author

Reiel Reinhart served over seven years in the Armed Forces and is a veteran. She aided the drawdown of the Iraqi War in 2011. Withstanding the winds of Time is her first collection of poems. On her off time you can find her writing, painting and taking photos of landscapes with her family in Central Massachusetts.

Reiel Reinhart

Author